William Harris Rule

Councils, Ancient and Modern

From the Apostolical Council of Jerusalem, to the Oecumenical Council of Nicaea, and to the last papal council in the Vatican

William Harris Rule

Councils, Ancient and Modern
From the Apostolical Council of Jerusalem, to the Oecumenical Council of Nicaea, and to the last papal council in the Vatican

ISBN/EAN: 9783337245993

Printed in Europe, USA, Canada, Australia, Japan

Cover: Foto ©ninafisch / pixelio.de

More available books at **www.hansebooks.com**

COUNCILS,

ANCIENT AND MODERN.

COUNCILS,

ANCIENT AND MODERN:

FROM THE

APOSTOLICAL COUNCIL OF JERUSALEM,

TO THE

ŒCUMENICAL COUNCIL OF NICÆA,

AND TO THE

LAST PAPAL COUNCIL IN THE VATICAN.

BY

WILLIAM HARRIS RULE, D.D.,

AUTHOR OF "THE HISTORY OF THE INQUISITION."

"Where the Spirit of the Lord is, there is Liberty."

LONDON:
HODDER AND STOUGHTON,
27, PATERNOSTER ROW.

MDCCCLXX.

PREFACE.

AFTER the interval of more than 300 years, the world hears again of an Œcumenical Council. To readers of ecclesiastical history the word is familiar, although it requires no low degree of ecclesiastical science to estimate with accuracy the relative importance of councils, and their value as registers of the state of society, and of the Church, at the times when they occur.

The object I have kept in view in this little book is, to present the general reader with a few characteristic notes, whereby he may be assisted to form some judgment of the Council now holding its sessions in Rome. If he pleases to study further, he may do so at his leisure, with the aid of more elaborate treatises. He may now compare it with that of Trent, which lingered through nearly twenty years, the rulers and representatives of the Church of Rome being all that time occupied in ostensible efforts to reform their Church and expound its doctrine, but in a real struggle to counteract the Evangelical Reformation, and to fortify their Church against the withering power of the truth and the merited indignation of society, long darkened and oppressed beneath its tyranny. Or he may compare it, assembled, as it is, under the sway of one Pope, with the Council of Constance, that disbanded several antipopes, set up in their stead a creature of their own, and comforted themselves with casting two martyrs into the flames before they separated. Or he may contrast this Council of the Vatican with the venerable Council of Nicæa, where there was no Pope at all, and where the one ruling motive of its members was a desire to search into the truth of Holy Scripture, to accept it with one consent, and then proclaim it to the world.

Always, and above all, recurring to the examples and instructions of Holy Scripture, the reader is invited to contemplate the unity of the Church of Christ, as represented by the 120 disciples, waiting with one accord in the upper chamber at Jerusalem to receive the Pentecostal blessing, and contrast therewith the disturbed company now brought together in the Vatican. Unlike the primitive disciples, the Cismontane and Ultramontane factions struggle with each other for ascendancy, and, in spite of every effort to keep their dissension secret, prove the impossibility of genuine concord so long as they are under the pressure of an anti-Christian authority, and are treated as the mere servants of one man, whom they have set up over themselves instead of Christ.

To diminish the mystery which, to many minds, obscures the idea of a council, I have taken care to mark what is most essential in the form and ceremonial of such assemblies.

There is one thing, I confess, which causes me greater surprise than anything as yet said or done by Pope Pius IX., or any person belonging to him; and that is, the general surprise, astonishment, and indignation which we Englishmen feel, or profess to feel, on the present occasion. The measure taken to accommodate the Church at Rome to the present state of things in the world, is but part of a course of action pursued steadily by its chief Pontiff and his advisers for nearly the quarter of a century. The thing itself is done exactly in the manner prescribed, with latest improvements, three centuries ago. The policy of profound secrecy; the absolute control; the denial of free debate, and the special ceremonies. The previous appointment of times for assembling the Council to receive and accept decrees and canons, without regard to time needed for due consideration or loss of time possible by inevitable delays; a supreme contempt of all things human, and a magnificent mockery of all that is Divine; these are not new features, nor do they arise from any peculiarity of character in the Pope. This whole affair has little personality in it. It is not attributable to the exuberance of genius, nor to the defect of wisdom in Pope or Court. It is the stubborn routine of a system of human machinery, that will work itself out until the weights are down. The machine fancies itself to be unchangeable, and so it is. It is a blind automaton, to be avoided while it holds together. It cannot be mended, and must be broken up.

The reader, it is hoped, will not complain because he does not find, within so small a space, information which is only to be gathered out of ponderous volumes, most of them written in a dead language, and scarcely ever opened except by hard-working canonists or studious antiquarians. It is presumed that nothing of the kind would be now desired.

W. H. R.

Croydon, Dec. 24th, 1869.

CONTENTS.

	PAGE
PREFACE	v
UNITY OF THE CHURCH OF CHRIST	11
EARLY CHRISTIAN COUNCILS	15
ŒCUMENICAL	21
COUNCILS FALSELY CALLED ŒCUMENICAL	31
THE COUNCIL OF TRENT	36
THE COUNCIL OF THE VATICAN	40
AVOWED OBJECTS OF THE POPE	54
"ERRORS" TO BE REMEDIED BY THE COUNCIL OF THE VATICAN	61
INFALLIBILITY	66
COUNCILS HELD IN ROME	73
PROBABLE EFFECTS OF THE LAST COUNCIL	76

FROM THE

APOSTOLICAL COUNCIL OF JERUSALEM,

TO THE

ŒCUMENICAL COUNCIL OF NICÆA,

AND TO THE LAST

PAPAL COUNCIL IN THE VATICAN.

Councils, Ancient and Modern.

UNITY OF THE CHURCH OF CHRIST.

Few persons in this country have any clear conception of what is meant by an Œcumenical Council. The last assemblage so called closed in the year 1563, and the world scarcely expected to see another. Some information on the subject may therefore be acceptable, and perhaps it cannot be conveyed more effectually than by surveying rapidly, yet with the greatest possible care, some of the councils noted in history from the commencement of Christianity until now.

Certainly there is no ill-meaning in the word, and the thing it represents may be very good or very bad. The Divine Head of the Church desired that we Christians should all be one, thinking and acting in concert. He separated

His first disciples from the world, constituted them one family, designed them to be a household of faith, and so described them collectively under various titles as to indicate their oneness. They were a flock, and He the shepherd; the Church a body, the Saviour of the Church its head; He the vine, Christians the branches; He the captain of their salvation, they good soldiers wearing the whole armour of God, wielding the sword of the spirit, and therewith withstanding every assault, and overcoming the world by faith. After His resurrection, He did not let the morning sun rise upon the hills around Jerusalem before He proceeded to gather together His dispersed family, and after the memorable forty days of intimate converse with them, He led them out together to Bethany, there to give them their commission to the world. He breathed on them the spirit of inspiration; He bade them go into the world and preach the Gospel to every creature; but even at that moment He imposed on them a most salutary restraint: " Tarry ye in Jerusalem until ye be endued with power from on high." For that power they were to pray, and go on praying until it came, for without it they would be weak and worthless. They obeyed their master, prayed, waited, and were of one accord in one place. So the best of the Saviour's followers were assembled for the single purpose of prayer, when the celestial flame descended, crowned each one of them with fire, and made them *fit* for united counsel, and then for united action. Their outward unity was not enough; neither would there be collective wisdom until each one of them came under the guidance of that inspiration of the Almighty which giveth understanding, not superseding study and care, but enabling His servants to judge and act aright in concert.

Now, this is not matter of speculation, but of history. It is well known that the early Christians were honourably distinguished from the masses of society around. Origen, whose name is to this day familiar, has a remarkable passage to our present purpose. He wrote less than two hundred years after our Lord's ascension into heaven, when Christianity had been long enough in the world to impress its heavenly character on many, and not long enough to have degenerated into superstition; and in his third book against Celsus, he appeals to the Greeks and Egyptians as witnesses of the superiority of Christian over heathen society. " The Churches of God," he said, " were well instructed, compared with the vulgar companies of men. They were evidently the lights of the world." He boldly contrasted the Christian congregations in Athens, Corinth, and Alexandria, cities which he well knew, with the civic assemblies in each of them, as being incomparably superior in intelligence, in manners, and in moral conduct, and then proceeds to say: "And if you examine the ecclesiastical senate of each of those cities, you will find some ecclesiastical senators fit to administer anywhere a divinely constituted commonwealth; but those senators whom you ordinarily meet with have nothing in their manners to distinguish them from the common people. The same of magistrates, who are members of our Churches, compared with their colleagues in civic authority, and who, although they discharge their duties with a certain air of coolness, far excel the other magistrates of the city and the ordinary senators in manners and in virtue."

We cannot doubt the truth of this representation. It exactly agrees with the language of St. Paul: "Dare any of you, having a matter against another, go to law before the unjust, and not before the saints? Do ye not know that the saints shall judge the world?" So long, however, as Christians were saints, Christian Councils were what they ought to be, but no longer. Before plunging into the troubled waters of later times, let us observe how ecclesiastical councils were conducted while the Church was pure.

EARLY CHRISTIAN COUNCILS.

PASSING by the election of Matthias, and the appointment of the Seven Deacons, let us fix our attention on what some call the First Council, or Council of Jerusalem, while they vainly wish to trace up the lineage of the councils that now are to that honourable parentage.

Twenty years had elapsed since the Resurrection of the Saviour. The chief men in the Church were beyond the age when zeal sometimes outruns judgment, and by various experience must have learned wisdom, and had attained to mature piety. At Antioch, the number of converts had greatly increased, and many of them were Gentiles. Some Jewish Christians came down from Judea, and taught that, unless they were circumcised after the manner of Moses, they could not be saved. This raised a grave question, which does not appear to have been mooted before, and the zealots pleaded what probably they felt,—the sincerity of a tender conscience. The Apostles resisted them, having a conscience no less tender, but far more enlightened; but while they well knew what to teach, they did not so well know what to do. Dissension wrought no good, and disputation made matters worse. Paul and Barnabas, with certain others of them, determined not to break the bond of charity, but went up together to Jerusalem to consult the Apostles and elders there. The Church brought them on their way. They preached Christ wherever they rested on their journey, " and when they were come to Jerusalem, they were received of the Church, and of the Apostles and elders, and declared the things that God had done with them." Then rose certain of the Pharisees, now believers in Christ, but severely rigid, and insisted that those converted Gentiles should be circumcised. No doubt their minds were somewhat ruffled, but so is the face of the ocean under an angry wind, and yet the depth of the ocean is unmoved. But "the Apostles and elders came together to consider of the matter." Having thus considered, they united in counsel with "the whole Church," and after earnest deliberation, conducted under the influence of wisdom superior to their own, the Apostles and elders and brethren sent back chosen men of their own company to Antioch with Paul and Barnabas, and wrote letters addressed to the brethren of the Gentiles in Antioch and Syria and Cilicia, with greeting from "the Apostles and elders and brethren," to tell them that "it seemed good to the Holy Ghost" and to themselves to lay upon them no greater burden than a very few necessary things, the observance of which would enable them to keep clear of Pagan defilements; but by no means would they trouble the Gentile converts with circumcision, nor with anything peculiar to the Mosiac Law, much less with Pharisaic traditions.

There was no ostentation of authority, no multitude of canons, no exaltation of either James or Simon, nor any hard words against their troublers. The effect of this godly wisdom was just what might have been expected. "When they," Paul and Barnabas, Barsabas and Silas, "were dismissed, they came to Antioch; and when they had gathered the multitude together, they delivered the Epistle, which, when they had read, they rejoiced with consolation." For "where the spirit of the Lord is, there is liberty."

Following this authoritative precedent, the Christians of that century and the two following took counsel together for the settlement of difficult questions, or for the remedy of evils that from time to time arose. For example, when Montanus, a Phrygian, a man self-willed and vain, fancied that he was the Paraclete, or Comforter, whom Christ had promised to send to His disciples, and endeavoured to assume the office of Patron or Protector of his fellows, several synods were assembled, to consult how that monstrous assumption might be disproved and ended. When Paul of Samosata denied the divinity of the Son of God and the personality of the Holy Ghost, many meetings, also called councils, were convened to consider how to counteract the error by a more effectual exhibition of the truth. When even the good Origen ran wild and spoiled his ministrations by the mixture of many follies, a council was held in Alexandria in Egypt for the same purpose.

Questions of discipline unavoidably arose. The Jewish members of the Church commemorated the death of Christ on the same day as the members of the Synagogue kept the Feast of the Passover. The Gentile Christians preferred to observe Easter, so that the Resurrection should always be commemorated on the first day of the week, not measuring the month from the new moon, as the Jews did. This difference of practice aggravated other differences, and let in upon the Church a spirit of caste which was very hurtful. Councils were, therefore, held in various places, especially in Cæsarea, Pontus, Rome, Corinth, and Ephesus.

In spite of the utmost watchfulness on the part of their pastors, many of the flock went astray, and even when conversions were most frequent, defections were probably most numerous; and there were many occasions of defection. But how far a wanderer might stray without passing quite beyond the pale of the Christian fold it was often difficult to tell, yet necessary to determine. For if a man were a Christian, he might admit a convert into the Church by baptism; but if he were not any more a Christian, it certainly would not be fitting that he should continue to meddle with the administration of a Christian sacrament, or pretend to admit others into a society he had himself deserted. Hence a keen controversy was carried on concerning baptism by heretics, and councils were consequently assembled in Africa, Italy, Cappadocia, and other parts of the world.

The propagation of the Gospel in Spain brought multitudes of Gentiles and Jews into the Church, who still hankered after their old idolatrous or sensual indulgences, or retained certain Jewish practices. It would appear that synods were very early holden in various parts of the Peninsula; and then in Elvira, near the site of Granada, as that city now stands, one large council was assembled about the year 306. The canons of that council, as they are now found, are very numerous, and it would be difficult to account for so large a collection at such an early date, apart from the conjecture that the bishops who met at Elvira brought with them canons which had been made in their several dioceses, and formed of them one collection; and the general tenor of those canons leads us to conclude—*first*, that the efforts of the early Spanish bishops had been directed to overcome prevailing vices, especially sins of licentiousness and savage passion; and, *secondly*, to counteract the influence of Judaism, which we know to have been very great indeed in that country, where Hebrews began to settle at least 1,300 years before. Even if those canons were written by the good men at Elvira just as we find them now, which is too much to be imagined, they show that, in spite of some slight approximation to the style of a century or two later, the Christian ministers of that age were earnest labourers, who sought to elevate the moral standard of society, and who would inflict the penance of abstinence, for example, upon immoral members of their congregations, with a sincere desire to humble them and do them good.

As yet, the councils have all been local, or, in the ecclesiastical acceptation of the word, provincial, except the Council of Elvira (*Elliberis*), which may be considered national, and bears evidence of the natural and proper tendency of Churches or congregations to unite for mutual succour or collective action. But it would scarcely have been possible to assemble a General Council to represent all Christendom so long as Christianity was treated as an illicit religion within the bounds of the empire, or, on its increase in numbers, received, at best, a cool and intermittent toleration. But a great change approaches on the conversion of an emperor to the Christian faith.

ŒCUMENICAL COUNCILS.

" IT came to pass in those days that there went out a decree from Cæsar Augustus, that all the world (πᾶσαν τὴν οἰκουμένην) should be taxed." *World* is the best word our translators could find in their incomparable Saxon to represent the Greek oikouměnē, which, in the language of the New Testament, meant *the empire*. That was a Roman boast. It was as if it had been said, "Wherever there stands a human habitation." So the Pope calls his domain the oikouměnē, and claims the largest acceptation for the name, pretending to spiritual sovereignty over all the globe. He, too, more ambitious than Augustus, would have the whole world to be taxed, and the present council is, with that understanding, called *œcumenical*.

In ecclesiastical style, at least in the Church of Rome, there are *Diocesan Synods*, consisting of the clergy of a diocese assembled and presided over by the bishop; Synods, or *Councils Provincial*, convened and presided over by the archbishop or metropolitan, a province being the territory that is, or is supposed to be, under the jurisdiction of an archbishop. A *National Council* consists of all the bishops of one nation, and an *Œcumenical Council* should consist of all the bishops in the world. Nothing less is meant by the ostentatious title, and no effort is spared to put a face of œcumenicity upon the assemblage now in Rome. It would require a distinct publication to show that the Greek and Oriental ecclesiastics who now make a figure there have no truly representative character, and that much of the parade of Greeks in this council is as dishonest as would be the stealing of a trademark in the world of commerce.

Using the word œcumenical as it was used in Greek, when the Roman Empire was in the height of its glory, it is equivalent with *imperial*. In that sense it was rightfully employed by Constantine the Great. The reader will remember that Constantine, when reigning over the western half of the Empire, went to war with his colleague, Licinius, Emperor of the eastern half. He conquered Licinius, and was much indebted for that conquest to the Christian soldiers in his army; attributed their bravery and their success to the succour of their God, granted in answer to their prayers. Licinius had persecuted the Christians, and now Constantine not only favoured them, but himself became a Christian.

At this time Arianism had broken out in the East, Arius being still alive and busy. The Arians were, in some parts of the Eastern Empire, the stronger party, and the orthodox Christians, on the fall of Licinius, appealed to Constantine for protection. Constantine, no less than Augustus, had the whole oikouměnē at his feet, and believing that the most reasonable way of reconciling adverse parties was to bring them face to face, invited the most eminent Christian ministers of East and West to come into his presence and debate the great question of our Lord's divinity. He was then at Nicomedia, a city of Bithynia, putting into order the affairs of the eastern portion of his united empire; and an assemblage of this kind was naturally and almost necessarily called œcumenical, or imperial. Of all Christian general councils, it was the *first* and *best*.

When Augustus issued his decree, the gates of the Temple of Janus, god of war, were shut, because the empire was at peace. When Constantine issued this summons to a council of Christian ministers, the temples of the Prince of Peace were all thrown open. War and persecution ceased at once. The schism of the empire was healed, and the victorious emperor desired to heal the schism of the Church.

At his command the invited members of the council were conveyed to Nicæa by sea and land. Ships and carriages, with every necessary comfort, were provided for them at the public charge. On their arrival at Nicæa, where they were to await the arrival of Constantine, they were honourably received as his friends. Whatever may be said to cast a reasonable doubt on

Œcumenical Councils. 25

his reported vision of a cross, and the story of the thundering legion, it is indisputably true that he attributed his possession of the entire empire to their prayers, and made no secret of his gratitude.

On a day appointed, in the year 325, about 300 confessors of Christ were assembled in a spacious apartment of his palace. Seats were placed around the hall, and the centre of the floor was clear. For the first time since the day of Pentecost a body of men, really representative of all Christendom, found themselves seated face to face in a chamber prepared for their occupation. It was not a dream, but a strange reality. They had met already in the Christian Church of Nicæa, and in presence of the congregation had given solemn thanks to God, and prayed for the power of the Holy Ghost to rest upon themselves in the expected discussion with Arius and his followers, and on the congregations of Europe, Asia, and Africa.

There was Alexander, the faithful Bishop of Alexandria, where Arius began to propagate his heresy, attended by a young deacon who became the champion of the faith for which they were now contending, and whose name passed into a proverb, " Athanasius against the world." There was Eustathius of Antioch, not unworthily surnamed the Great, a man of signal eloquence, and a veteran confessor during the persecution of Licinius, if not also of Diocletian, venerable for piety and learning; Macarius, shepherd of the Christian flock in Jerusalem, the scene of our Saviour's humiliation and of His triumph too, chiefly hated, as well became him, by the deniers of the Lord's Divinity. Cæcilian came from Carthage, strong in the faith. Menophantes, from Byzantium, had stood unshaken under Arian persecution. From Thebais, in Egypt, the aged Paphnutius, eminent for his resistance of the first proposal to impose celibacy on his brethren, he being himself unmarried, in consequence of life-long suffering for the cause of Christ, in which he never would involve a wife. James of Nisibis, in Mesopotamia. The learned Leontius of Cæsarea, in Cappadocia, teacher of Gregory Nazianzum, and many others, whose names are less famous, but whose labours rendered them well worthy of the distinction they received. Alexander of Thessalonica, by whom Athanasius, when in the height of his well-earned honours, was pleased to be called his "son." Osius, the wise and devoted Bishop of Cordova, the Nestor, in his time, of Christian counsels. Victor of Rome sent two to represent him, Vitus and Vincent. Persia, Armenia, and Scythia sent representatives.

Many of these men bore marks of the suffering they had undergone. One had lost an eye under the hand of the tormentor, and was maimed on one side. Many bore scars of wounds received in like manner, and others were bending under premature age in consequence of hunger, care, and excessive labour in their Master's work.

A golden chair was ready for the Emperor, and on a table before it lay a copy of the Gospels, or perhaps of the entire Bible. No crucifix, no symbol, no lighted lamps on that bright 19th day of June. The loathsomeness of idolatry had been too lately tasted. Space was left for the imperial attendants, and Arius and his party also had places found them with their brethren, if brethren they might be.

All being ready, Constantine sent some of his servants to announce his approach. They were not armed guards, but Christians selected from his body guard, and without their arms. The "Fathers" rose in silence as the Emperor himself entered. He came in his purple, glittering with jewels and heavy with gold; at once bearing on his person the sign of imperial pomp and the badge of Roman degeneracy. Yet, unlike his predecessors, he bowed reverently in presence of the servants of that God who has no other image on earth than such a likeness of Himself as, by His grace, those servants can exhibit. They say he blushed. He might have thought of the wrongs the good men had suffered. He might have felt the power of the Holy Spirit, whose presence they had sought. Eusebius, the historian, was there, and, as eye-witness, describes the bearing of Constantine at that moment, and so affords us a glance which almost reveals the working of that Spirit of Truth which, above emperor and bishops, presided at the first Council of Nicæa.

There is not room here for any adequate account of the proceedings of this council. Canons attributed to it may be found in the collections of the Acts of Councils, but the most trustworthy accounts must be sought in the writings of Eusebius and Athanasius. Sozomen and Theodoret are secondary authorities, and Philostorgius is inferior still. The chief monument of the Council is the Nicene Creed, so far as the words, "I believe in the Holy Ghost." Some spurious canons, now added to the canons of a Council held at Sardica, twenty-two years later, but not really adopted at that Council, are intended to represent that the Bishop of Rome should be appealed to in any case where councils cannot agree. These canons were never acknowledged by the Universal Church, nor made use of by any but the popes. But the Council of Nice was truly œcumenical, and can be mentioned with honour and thankfulness. It was convened by a Christian Emperor on an appeal from his own subjects before popes existed, and when the Bishop of Rome had not yet attempted to assume the position of Supreme Pastor of the Universal Church. That usurpation came to pass nearly three centuries later.

The Œcumenical Council of Constantinople in the years 381-383, finished the work begun at Nicæa. It was summoned from the whole empire, both east and west, by the Emperor Theodosius. The Confession of Faith in the Holy Ghost in the Nicene Creed was found scarcely sufficient to represent the prevailing faith of Christians or the statements of Holy Scripture, and therefore the following words were added at Constantinople :—

"And I believe in the Holy Ghost, the Lord and giver of Life, who proceeded from the Father, who, with the Father and the Son, together is worshipped and glorified ; who spake by the Prophets. And I believe one Catholic and Apostolic Church. I acknowledge one baptism for the remission of sins, and I look for the resurrection of the dead, and the life of the world to come." Soon afterwards, the doxology, "Glory be to the Father, and to the Son, and to the Holy Ghost," with the response, "As it was in the beginning, is now, and ever shall be, world without end, Amen," was added to the perpetual confession of Christendom, and has resounded in the true Catholic Church ever since. With this closes what we have to say concerning the councils properly called Œcumenical.

COUNCILS FALSELY CALLED ŒCUMENICAL.

APART from the proceedings of a council, whether good or evil, its title to be called universal, or œcumenical, simply depends on the decision of one question, whether or not it contains, so far as may be possible, representatives of the Christian Church in all parts of the world, and of all the recognised divisions of the Church of Christ. So vast and various an assemblage could scarcely be hoped for, and, if it were possible, it is certain that it could not act. Even if it acted, the character of its proceedings would have to be ascertained before the world could possibly know how to estimate its value. Therefore, taking no account of the name, it remains to ascertain whether the so-called General Councils, which have been held since the times of Nicæa and Constantinople to the present, have been such as to deserve the confidence or gratitude of posterity.

The Second Council of Nicæa, for example, convened at the bidding of the Empress Irene in the year 787, for the express purpose of establishing the worship of images in the churches of the East, after the images had been broken by the zeal of the people, and under the sanction of a numerous council assembled in Constantinople, can only be mentioned as having upheld idolatry and dishonoured the Christian name. In relation to the history of Europe, it is marked as the proximate cause of separating east and west; and they who can see God in history fail not to notice the retribution which makes the division of Europe in the eighth century a chief cause of the gradual weakening of the Latin Church from that time to the present. Very soon after the decrees of the second council of Nicæa, for the restoration of "sacred images" in churches and elsewhere, the Greek Church formally separated from the Church of Rome, and now treats its overtures for reconciliation with dignified disdain. The second council of Nicæa was, after all, more political than religious; and the history of those assemblies is full of evidence to show that contentious priests and rival princes were playing with the sacred interests of mankind and desecrating the name of Christianity. All experience, therefore, after the fourth century of the Christian era, teaches that the religion of the Saviour was framed and established by Himself, and that there is no Parliament of any sort, either civil or ecclesiastical, that can frame it anew, or that mankind can trust to improve or strengthen it.

A remarkable period in the history of such assemblies extends from the Council of Pisa to that of Basil in the fifteenth century.

Curious collectors of dates and facts count no fewer than six-and-twenty schisms in the Church of Rome, that is to say, divisions of the whole popedom into separate "obediences." Seven of these, however, took place before the Bishop of Rome became Pope by the express authority of the Emperor Phocas. Nineteen times since then, two or more antipopes have been contending for the occupation of the Papal throne, each of them having the title of Pope, and receiving homage as such from a portion of the popedom. At length the case of the Papacy became desperate, and it was to be apprehended that as Constantinople and Rome were irrecoverably separated, so Rome and Avignon, each having its own pope, with his cardinals and court, the schism of Christendom would be permanent, and the Papacy itself eventually become impossible. The Councils of Pisa, Constance, and Basil spent about thirty-five years in striving, not quite unsuccessfully, to save the Papacy, but with no regard to what is most essential to the unity and safety of the Church of God.

While two antipopes, under the names of Benedict XIII. and Gregory XII. were struggling for ascendancy, the cardinals of the two obediences were met in the Cathedral of Pisa to assume the government of the divided Church, and sit in judgment over both of them. Both were summoned to appear, but neither came. Thrice a cardinal made solemn proclamation at the church-door, but they were contumacious notwithstanding. After due solemnity, they were solemnly proclaimed contumacious and heretical, and a successor to the throne was elected and adored under the name Alexander V.

Alexander was utterly worthless; he soon died,

and was succeeded by one of his patrons. Forthwith *the Council of Constance* assembled, in the year 1414, under the Emperor Sigismund, and had much work to do in getting rid of three antipopes and creating one new Pope, who took the name of Martin V. But the three false pontiffs, John XXIII., Gregory XII., and Benedict XIII., were not the only troubles of the notorious Council of Constance. Two heretics, namely, John Huss and Jerome of Prague, were spreading doctrines more hated by the members of the Council than all the antipopes, with their vicious habits and restless greed. They had learned the doctrine promulgated by our John Wycliffe, and the kingdom of Bohemia threatened to cast off the Papacy, now made so utterly contemptible. The Council, therefore, divided its cares between the affairs of the antipopes and those of the heretics. Huss they summoned into their presence, and he came thither under a safe conduct from the Emperor; but no sooner did they get him within the gates of Constance than they took him into custody, passed him from prison to prison, tried him for heresy, and finally bound him to a stake and burnt him alive. A noble Bohemian who boldly came to Constance to plead for him, undaunted by the prospect of a cruel death, was in like manner

Councils falsely called Œcumenical. 35

seized, imprisoned, convicted of heresy, and burnt alive. Having set up a new Pope and martyred two witnesses for God's truth, the Council of Constance dispersed, and its name became a brand of infamy.

Still the schism continued; no council ever burnt a Pope, or a pretender to the Popedom, and therefore none of these Gregories or Benedicts came to the stake. They lived on, others sprang up after them, and at length another Council met at Basil, where it laboured vainly for many years to heal the system, but proved the incapacity of such Councils to do anything but mischief. It remained in permanence from 1431 to 1443, and dissolved itself with two pontiffs more firmly than ever settled in their seats. One of them, Nicholas V., having better temper and sounder sense than most of his predecessors, so far outmatched his competitor Felix, as to induce him to put off the habit of a Pope, and accept that of a cardinal, with wealth and quietness to the end of his days. Much more was not heard of those useless gatherings until the lapse of another century, when the Council of Trent was obtained on the earnest demand of some of the Sovereigns of Europe, and others, who trusted that something might be done to satisfy those who desired the Reformation of the Church and Court of Rome.

THE COUNCIL OF TRENT.

THE history of the Council of Trent is better known to general readers than that of any other. Very briefly, therefore, let it be noted that it met in the 1545, and, after many suspensions and much delay, closed its last and busiest session on December 4th, 1563. The council, be it first of all observed, was completely under the control of the Pope, his cardinals, and Italian priests. The Italians were always able to command a majority if questions were to be settled by mere majority of votes; but votes were not free, and we shall presently see very distinctly that in such a council freedom is impossible.

The object chiefly pursued was to counteract the Protestant Reformation. To that end the council endeavoured to silence the complaints of the laity in general, and of a few of the most estimable of the Romish clergy, by a reformation of their own. Some gross abuses and irregularities were, no doubt, corrected; and an entire system of ecclesiastical government was constructed with a view to improve the character

Council of Trent. 37

of the clergy in general, and enable them to cope with the reformed churches in Germany, France, and England. Scandals could thenceforth be more easily diminished or concealed from common observation. The doctrine to be professed by the Romish theologians was also very carefully considered. The canons relating to doctrine were drawn up with consummate care by men whom better education qualified for the work. We must remember that the closing of the great schism and the revival of letters were contemporaneous events, and that the earliest and most important labours of the printing press were carried on with ever-increasing vigour, together with the advances of the Protestant Reformation, in the period that intervened between the Council of Basil and the close of the Council of Trent. Men of superior knowledge and great talent who arose under the light of that Reformation promoted the culture of new science, and laboured hard to clothe the Church in new habiliments, and to administer her government with a more sagacious policy. All this must be freely acknowledged, and ought to be clearly understood; but, at the same time, even the most liberal charity has no veil that she can cast over the essential barbarism of the Church of Rome, which no degree of intellectual culture in its rulers can altogether overcome. Take the concluding acclamations with which the "Fathers of the Council" made known their sentiments.

After the Cardinal Morone, first legate, had pronounced his benediction, and bidden them depart in peace, the Cardinal De Lorraine read aloud:—

"To the most blessed Pope Pius, our Lord, and pontiff of the holy and universal Church, many years and eternal memory."

The fathers responded:—

"O Lord God, preserve our most holy Father long time to thy Church; many years!"

Card. "To the souls of the most blessed supreme pontiffs, Paul III. and Julius III., by whose authority this holy general council was begun, peace from the Lord, and eternal glory, and felicity in the light of the saints.

Resp. "May their memory be blessed!"

Card. "Blessed be the memory of Charles V., Emperor, and of the most serene kings who promoted and protected this universal council.

Resp. "Amen! Amen!"

Card. "To the most serene Emperor Ferdinand, ever august, orthodox, and pacific, and to all our kings, commonwealths, and princes, many years.

Resp. "O Lord, preserve the pious and Christian Emperor: O Heavenly Emperor, keep thou the earthly kings that are preservers of the right faith.

Card. "Great thanks to the legates of the Apostolic See, with many years.

Resp. "Great thanks. The Lord reward them!

Card. "To the most reverend cardinals, and illustrious orators.

Resp. "Great thanks; many years!

Card. "Life to the most holy bishops, and a happy return to their churches.

Resp. "Perpetual memory to the preachers of the truth! Many years to the orthodox senate.

Card. "The Sacrosanct Council of Trent: let us confess its faith; let us always keep its decrees!

Resp. "Let us ever confess: let us ever keep.

Card. "We all thus believe. We all think the same thing. We all consent; and, accepting, we all subscribe. This is the faith of Blessed Peter, and of the Apostles. This is the faith of the Fathers. This is the faith of the orthodox.

Resp. "So we believe. So we think. So we subscribe.

Card. "While we adhere to these decrees, we

shall be rendered worthy of the mercies and grace of our great High Priest, Jesus Christ, God; our holy ever-virgin Lady, the mother of God, and all saints at the same time interceding.

Resp. "So be it. So be it. Amen! Amen!

Card. "A curse upon all heretics.

Resp. "A curse! A curse!"

The solemn anathema rang through Europe, and the decrees of the Council, with all its acts, provoked much dissatisfaction. Philip II. of Spain, whose memory in England, as husband of "Bloody Queen Mary," has no honour, accepted the Council, not deigning to consult the wishes of his subjects, with whom it was exceedingly unpopular. The rulers of other states followed very tardily; but France, from that day to this, has not accepted the Council of Trent. Some of the most eminent of the French clergy have written elaborate treatises in opposition to Ultramontanism, in relation to the present council.

THE COUNCIL OF THE VATICAN.

As matters now stand, there is no country in the old world where a place could be found for the assemblage of a general council, with its traditional display, in connection with the Church of Rome, beyond the little province wherein the City of Rome stands. There, and only there, the Pope and his cardinals can do nearly as they please. In obedience to the Papal summons, which bears date June 29th, 1868, a considerable number of patriarchs, archbishops, and bishops, with the heads of monastic orders, and other ecclesiastical dignitaries, are met together. As for those that are resident in Rome, they are present, of course, and are the chief actors; many who bear high titles have no more than the titles to give them seats in a council of bishops, as their sees and patriarchates exist only in imagination, they being only what is called *in partibus*—titular bishops and even patriarchs of cities and countries, where they neither do nor can reside. Therefore, they who have gone to Rome from many parts of the world, have not all been influenced by reverence and fidelity to the Pope, as many persons fancy, but, as Archbishop Manning truly says, they were not invited, but summoned, having been previously bound by oath to go to Synod when called for. Every bishop elect, before he can be consecrated, must swear to these words:—*Vocatus ad Synodum veniam, nisi præpeditus fuero canonicâ præpeditione.* "When called to a Synod I will come, unless I shall be hindered by a canonical hindrance." And, whether summoned or not, he promises in the same oath that at certain periods, which are fixed according to the distance of his diocese from Rome, he will present himself at the threshold of the Apostles, that is to say, before the Pope at Rome, to give an account of his proceedings in the service of His Holiness.

The present Council was to meet on the 8th December, 1869; but even that precise appointment produced a false impression on those who did not know that the business of the Council would be, in reality, transacted before that day. Dr. Manning refers to this fact, in the Pastoral Letter which he sent to his clergy in England, previously to his own departure. "You are already aware," he says, "that the preparatory congregations are seven in number, and that the matters distributed to them comprehend *faith, philosophy, discipline, the relations of the Church with civil society, education, and the like.*" This gives no clue to the actual allotment of business to the seven congregations (or committees), nor to the names of the persons of whom they consisted, nor to the times of their sitting, nor the manner of transacting business, nor the presidents appointed to manage them. But we are sure that such congregations are always placed under the direction of men whom the Pope nominates, and who act under his orders. One thing, however, should be noted well, and it cannot be better stated than in the words of the pastoral now quoted : " None but those who are admitted to the work of preparing for the Council know what is in preparation ; and they are all bound by the Pontifical secret. From them nothing can be known ; from others nothing can be learned. As St. Augustine said, '*Nemo dare potest quod non habet.*' "

The public proceedings, or ceremonies, have been abundantly described by newspaper correspondents, and need not be repeated here. They were all substantially the same as are prescribed in the "Roman Pontifical" and "Ceremonial of Bishops." The order of the first spectacle on the 8th of December, as laid down in those books, was punctually followed. The procession, the mass, the special prayers, &c., and the allocution, were all according to the books. As to allocution, it has been translated from Latin into English, and circulated in our daily newspapers ; but one passage attracted special attention and remark, as well it might. The Pope read the allocution before the vast assemblage in St. Peter's, and closed a passage descriptive of the state of the world, as he views it, with these startling words :—

"But as St. John Chrysostom said, '*Nothing is more powerful than the Church; the Church is stronger than heaven itself.*' 'Heaven and earth shall pass away, but my words shall not pass.' What words? 'Thou art Peter, and on this rock I shall build my Church, and the gates of hell shall not prevail against it.'"

The present writer no sooner read this passage than he perceived that it was *intended* to convey the impression that Chrysostom had so explained our Lord's words in one of his homilies, and accordingly turned to the volume of Saville's Chrysostom, where it is to be found; and he now presents a careful translation of the original text, that the reader may compare the two, and judge of the Pope's honesty—if the Pope knows Greek, or his credulity if he does not. In the 77th Homily on the Gospel according to St. Matthew the passage referred to stands thus:—

"*Heaven and earth shall pass away, but my words shall not pass away:*

"That is to say, these things, which are compact and immoveable, shall more easily vanish out of sight than that aught of my words shall fail. And let him who speaks against them test the sayings, and when he finds the truth,—for he surely shall find it,—let him believe in the things which are to come by those which have passed away. Let him also search out all things with care, and he will see that the end of the events bears witness to the truth of prophecy. *And he directed their attention to the elements (τὰ δὲ στοιχεῖα εἰς μέσον τεθείκεν), at the same time pointing out that the Church is far more precious (προτιμοτέρα) than heaven and earth together, and showing that He himself is creator of the whole.*"

As for the pretended allusion to the words of our Lord concerning St. Peter, let the reader refer to the sacred text (Matt. xxiv.), and ascertain for himself whether there is any such allusion. The false statement in the allocution gives a poor idea of the Pope's alleged infallibility; yet, if we may trust to the insight which Dr. Manning may be presumed to have, it is intended that the Council shall declare it to be an article of faith. Whether or not such a declaration be made in this Council of the Vatican, it is not only in the belief, but in the practice of the Court of Rome that such infallibility is acknowledged.

There is an elaborate code of law for Rome itself (*De Ordine procedendi in Judiciis in Romanâ Curiâ Praxis Recentior*), which contains in its preface, word by word, the following declaration:—

"He is Vicar of God, and takes his place in the world (*vicegerens in terris*). He is God on earth, who judges all men, and is judged of no man; whose judgment God reserves without question to his own discretion. His most ample power no mortal can restrain. In him no defect of power is admitted, for he can do all things, and to doubt of his power is a crime and sacrilege. The power and jurisdiction which are given to himself of God he frequently exercises by himself. Nor does the Supreme Pontiff exercise this jurisdiction by himself only, but he exercises it also by others, and grants the same also to divers judges, as well in the city [Rome] as in the world—that is to say, to legates, by virtue of office (*nati*), or to legates whom he sends (*de latere*); to the patriarchs, archbishops, bishops, and all prelates of the whole world; as well as to the governors of the Ecclesiastical State, and the other judges of the Court of Rome."

Such is the language of the temporal power in Rome, where Pius IX. is king, and where his absolute supremacy is not merely a pretension, but a practical reality. The doctrine laid down in the civil law of Rome and the Roman State speaks in the very words now quoted; and out of the meshes of the law, of which this doctrine of the Pope's divine and absolute authority is the soul, there is no escape, and beyond it there can be no appeal. The members of the Council voluntarily cast themselves into the grasp of the Roman Government, and are helplessly self-surrendered to its mercy. To put away the last atom of hope that any one of them might otherwise entertain of being allowed to think, or speak, or act for himself in congregation or in council, the Pope, on the first day of this Council, received his oath, as we may gather from the notices of the ceremonial. Every one of them was made swear to the words appointed in the *Ordo ad Synodum* in the Roman Pontifical to the following effect :—

"I, N——, promise and swear true obedience to the Roman pontiff, successor of the blessed Peter, prince of the apostles, and Vicar of Jesus Christ. Without any doubt, I also receive and profess all other things delivered, defined, and declared by the sacred canons and œcumenical councils, and especially by the most holy Synod of Trent. *And at the same time I equally condemn, reject, and curse, all things contrary, and whatsoever heresies are condemned, rejected, and cursed by the Church.* This true Catholic faith, without which no man can be saved, which at this time I freely profess and truly hold, the same will I be careful, God helping, to retain entire and inviolate, most constantly, to the last breath of my life, *and will cause to be confessed, held, taught, and preached by my subjects, and by those for whom it devolves on me to care.* I, the said N——, promise, vow, and swear, so help me God and these holy Gospels of God."

This oath has been administered; and men who have been sworn in at this rate, however much they may seem to talk in their lodgings, or in the congregations that are now meeting, or in the Council itself—whatever they may dare to say under protestation of obedience reserved—are not free. There can be no freedom of speech beyond the limit of the Council of Trent, or of any ecclesiastical authority that may be quoted against them. Their lips will be sealed, whenever the presiding legate declares that it is his pleasure for them to be silent. They must say and do as they are commanded, or take the consequences. They have sworn obedience to the Pope as head of the Council and ruler of the world. They have also taken his command not to quit Rome without his permission until the Council is dissolved; and they have neither protection nor deliverance from his control, so long as their enforced attendance lasts. And yet their master complains dolorously if any one interferes with *his liberty* to bind and flog his slaves, even though they be rightfully the subjects of other Sovereigns.

On the day following, there was another procession and another ceremony in St. Peter's, and the only thing done by the Fathers was then to walk into the Council Chamber, receive information of what matters would now be laid before them for their consideration, and of the day when the Council should meet again. The *Second* Session having been thus disposed of, the *Third* was to be on the 6th day of January following. Meanwhile, congregations were to meet, and to prepare their conclusions, if any, on the subjects committed to their wisdom. The wisdom of the congregations would be to decide according to the pleasure of the Pope and his legates, and the duty of the Council to meet on the Epiphany would be for each Father distinctly to pronounce his *placet*, and so be content, according to the tenor of his oath.

The proceedings of the congregations were to be secret, and the reports of the short-hand writers to be sealed up from public observation. The Congregation of the Inquisition no doubt still exists in Rome, that privileged spot on earth, where Secrecy holds her undisputed sway, Justice and Mercy embrace each other in obedient slumber, that nothing may interrupt the action of that god upon earth whose pleasure it is a crime and a sacrilege to thwart, or even to dispute.

The only comfort for an outspoken member of a congregation, if such there be, must arise from the hope that the days of burning are past; but as the Castle of St. Angelo has not yet been dealt with as was the Castle of the Bastille, and the cells of St. Angelo are said to be both dark and deep, the fear of starvation or of immuration is not altogether groundless; and as the discourses in congregation may implicate others besides the speakers, there is no knowing what may be the consequences to other parties now in Rome. The regimen and customs of the dark ages being revived, the gates of the city and the frontiers of the little State of the Church being well guarded for the present, the trap is dangerous.

One distinguishing feature of this Council of the Vatican is, the perfection of the "Pontifical Secret." In all former Councils the Sovereigns and Governments of the world have had their representatives, and although those representatives were, latterly at least, ecclesiastics bound to the Pope by canonical obedience, they were also bound to their worldly masters, who had some choice of their own in sending them, and could recall them at any moment. Then, however skilfully they might try to temporise, they had to deal with other statesmen perhaps as clever as themselves. The trains of these "Orators," too, were full of curious observers and accomplished spies. Few of the Fathers themselves were quite incorruptible, and Princes present in the city being surrounded by their own servants, political secrecy was almost impossible. Nation checked nation.

Not so now. There is not a single acknowledged representative of any prince or state, and the political persons present are themselves of the least estimable kind, entirely sympathising with the falling papacy, and ready to help it in the way of mischief to any extent practicable. But no public servant, in whom the people of any country could confide, is employed to treat with the assembled Council openly and in good faith. The secret, therefore, will be kept with tenfold vigour, and held fast, to the prejudice, if possible, of society at large. That which, in past ages, has been the destruction that wasteth at noon-day, will now be openly "the pestilence that walketh in darkness." Half the terror, therefore, is gone, and a free diffusion of light is all that is wanted to dispel the other half.

In all this mass of secrecy there must be much that is intangible, and will never be brought out into daylight. Every pressing interest of Romanism will, of course, gain the most intense and full attention, quite apart from Council or congregation either; and for anything we can even conjecture to the contrary, the topics ostensibly submitted to them for examination in their very brief and intermittent meetings, will be but secondary to other matters that will keep some men busy night and day, quite apart from the routine of Council. Meanwhile, session after session may take place without any business at all being transacted. The Fathers may show themselves on a day appointed, and after some prayers and chanting, with a mass and a sermon, may adjourn for weeks or months, and so keep up the face of a Council, while the Court of Rome carries on its bye-play on any variety of subjects, without letting the world hear a whisper of intelligence. This was done at the Council of Trent, for the sake of gaining time and wearing out opposition; but now, for the reason already stated, the Court of Rome has a broader and clearer field for secret and independent action, and may not care for such delay.

And this is not mere suspicion. It has been necessarily made known for the information of intending perverts, that the Pope is acting for himself in their business, without any participation of the Council, and will communicate with bishops or priests not in communion with Rome, or with persons not now acknowledged by Rome as such, but who conceive their orders to be valid. They are told that he appoints pious and prudent men to confer with them, hear their grievances, consider their case, and, where it is possible, devise methods for removing hindrances out of the way, and, by any possible concession, supplying what is defective. Where the confidential agents thus appointed can present any ministers of the Church of England, for example, who might be worth having, the Pope, in the plenitude of his power, may impart to such persons the qualification for ministering at the altar which they do not yet possess, and thus may engage many unfortunate clerics whose defective *orders* as Protestants, or whose imperfect *state* as married men, would be a barrier insurmountable to any council, and assist them to cast themselves at once upon his clemency. He might even create them Bishops, and lead them rejoicing into the next session of the Council. The Council might sing a *Te Deum* over a few such converts in the arch-cathedral of the Catholic world—perhaps over many such—

and so take a long stride nearer to that happy state of reconciliation so long anticipated for this land of *Angeli*. Perhaps, in reward for bringing about a far inferior transformation, the Triple Crown itself might be placed upon the head of the former Anglican Archdeacon, who has been chosen to convey the enticing information to his Anglican brethren in this country.

AVOWED OBJECTS OF THE POPE.

NOTWITHSTANDING the Pontifical secret which shrouds every detail, hides the progress of affairs from the public eye, and enables the Pope and his friends to delay or expedite, to relinquish or persevere, as circumstances may require, there are some cherished aspirations of Pius IX. which it is morally certain he will not now surrender.

His ambition to crush the spirit of nationality in Italy was rebuked early in his pontificate. He had seen that it was no longer possible to resist openly the operation of that spirit, and therefore attempted to beguile the Italian patriots, by professing to be himself a patriot and a liberal. The dissimulation would be a virtue to the apprehension of one who can favour Jesuitism for its maxim of doing evil *in majorem gloriam Dei;* and if mankind were altogether so dim-sighted as mediæval discipline would make them, he might have succeeded ; but his doings were discovered. The Pontifical secret was broken by the pontiff himself, who intrigued with the Austrian too recklessly, and his career of political conspiracy against the liberties of Europe was cut short by that ignominious conflict with the subjects of his own state, which made it impossible for him to attain eminence in this particular sphere of reactionary politics.

He turned towards other subjects on which his talents could be more effectually employed, and, as yet, not without some success. His aims are clearly ascertained, and may be described in very few words. He would bring up the dogma of his Church to the full standard of absurdity. He would regain for the Church the power over society which it has nearly lost.

First, as to dogma. The " pious opinion" of an immaculate conception of the Virgin Mary had prevailed among the devotees of some monastic orders, and had served to confirm the weaker minds in Mary-worship. To recover the fanatics, after he had lost the liberals, would be a consolatory compensation, and he spared no pains to gain it. A request to all the bishops to give him their judgment on the expediency of declaring the opinion to be a veritable dogma, put him into correspondence with the whole episcopate, when he managed to gain their views, evade their difficulties, and overrule the objections of some of them; by a stroke of prerogative, and the exercise of a little canonical severity, he raised the profane fable to the desired standard of an article of faith.

The spectacle of December 8, 1854, in Rome, gave him encouragement to proceed in the same path. In the mind of the superstitious masses he was associated with the new honours of the "mother of God" and 10,000 preaching zealots were thenceforth made his panegyrists. The 8th of December was the day set apart in honour of the Immaculate Conception of the Blessed Virgin, first definitely proclaimed by His Holiness Pope Pius IX.

This point gained, a second might fairly be contemplated—to make the infallibility of the Pope himself an article of faith binding upon all "Catholics," or, if we must speak in the Roman manner, binding upon all mankind. The rumour that it was intended to call upon the Council to accept the dogma roused the opposition of multitudes in all parts of the world, but especially in France. Nearly two centuries ago the Gallican clergy protested against the claims of the Popes to be acknowledged infallible, and absolute masters of all bishops. The protest was supported by the learning of the Sorbonne, by the authority of the King, and by the common sense of the French people. To make it obligatory on all persons to *profess* to believe—for believe they cannot—that the Popes are infallible, whether speaking ordinarily or officially, *ex cathedra*, would now endanger an open secession of the French people and clergy from the Roman see; and already Monsignor Maret, Bishop of Sura, and Dean of the Faculty of Theology in Paris, has written against the doctrine of the supremacy and infallibility of the Popes, and promises to write again on the same subject after the Council closes. He has gone to Rome with the understanding that he will oppose the addition of this dogma to the creed; and others have allowed it to be understood that they will sustain him in their opposition. But the terms of the oath, which has been partly copied in a preceding page, are so clearly in accord with the notion of an absolute and unerring perfection in the Pope, that some thought it improbable that the proposal would ever be submitted to the Council for acceptance, but only announced in the hearing of the Council, that some of the fathers previously engaged or instructed to that effect might, by acclamation, signify assent. Hired acclamation of loyalty and venal votes are so common in Rome that nothing would be easier than to buy such an acclamation with silver, and that this aged ecclesiastic, like Herod, should accept worship as a god. The Ultramontanists might please themselves in shouting, "It is the voice of a god, and not of a man;" but it is hardly possible that the other division of Romanism, usually called Cismontane, would join in chorus.

Second, as to the relations of the Church of Rome to society at large, the ambition of this pontiff led him to expect, many years ago, that he might earn for himself the signal honour of overturning European society to its foundations, and he has not made any secret of his marvellous delusion.

Five years ago, "the Pope's printers" in Paris were employed to publish a volume containing "a collection of all the Consistorial Allocutions, Encyclicals, and other Apostolic Letters of the Sovereign Pontiffs Clement XII., Benedict XIV., Pius VI., Pius VII., Leo XII., Gregory XVI., and Pius IX., that are cited in the Encyclical and

Syllabus of 8th December, 1864," with other documents. This remarkable volume, put forth under the sanction of Pius IX., chiefly consists of writings issued by himself, and conveying a solemn condemnation of the principles, both good and bad, that prevail in various circles of modern society. There is, last of all, a "Syllabus of Errors," wherein those principles or opinions are categorically expressed, and denounced with all the force of language which the writers of ecclesiastical censures have at their command. A cursory perusal of the Syllabus with reference to the documents out of which it is constructed, shows that the sentences uttered by the present Pope are by no means expressive of any peculiarly intense bigotry in himself, but of a steady purpose, entertained from the beginning of his reign, if not before, to combat the obnoxious propositions which the majority of intelligent persons maintain, both out of the Church of Rome and in it. Perhaps to conceal his one chief intention, he enumerates, first of all, the most revolting blasphemies of infidelity.

Turning from the Syllabus and the mass of documentary matter by aid of which it is to be more fully understood, and referring to the Letters Apostolic by which the present "Œcumenical Council" is proclaimed, we find that Pius IX.

proposes that this Council shall weigh and determine what is to be done, that "by God's good help," as he says, "all evils may be removed from the Church and from civil society; that unhappy wanderers may be brought back into the straight path of truth, justice and salvation; that, *vices and errors* being taken away, our august religion and its salutary doctrine may receive fresh life."

Now the "*vices and errors*" are specified in the Syllabus, last in the collection of Allocutions and Letters now referred to; and on examining the public acts and manifestoes of the Pope from his accession in 1846 to the Letters Apostolic of 1864, convening this Council of 1869, we trace the progress of his efforts from year to year, in order to accomplish one great design. The unflinching determination he has displayed from the beginning is to be accounted for by the fact that none of his ideas are new. He is only doing his utmost to carry out the intention of his Church; of which intention the Popes whose names are enumerated, were, in their time, exponents. And this Council of the Vatican, closely following in the steps of the Council of Trent, is intended to assist the principle of absolute authority, as it was maintained by the most strongly ambitious pontiffs of ages past.

The vices, of course, are all worthy of condemnation; some of the errors ought to be regarded with abhorrence, and many others with decided disapproval; but many "errors," as they are called in the Syllabus, are in reality the principles of Evangelical Reformation, of civil and religious liberty, and of social justice and humanity. These the Popes and Court of Rome have always assailed with their utmost power, while gross vices and soul-destroying errors have been dealt with very tenderly, and drawn forth little more than feeble remonstrances, which hint connivance while they speak displeasure. As the Council is to try again what the Church of Rome can do against those errors, let us note a few of them.

"ERRORS" TO BE REMEDIED BY THE COUNCIL OF THE VATICAN.

It has been intimated by advocates of this Council that, as the Supreme Pontiff has defined and condemned the errors of the Syllabus, it would become the Council to affirm the contrary propositions. It could not be possible, they say, for a Council, being far inferior to a Pope, to confirm his sentence by any act of theirs, but they could respectfully echo his voice by pronouncing truth, just the contrary of the errors he condemns. Let us try the extremely simple process, and see what would be the "*truths*" propagated in England and in the whole British empire under the seal of Roman infallibility. The *errors* shall be marked with Roman numerals, as in the Syllabus (XIX., etc.), and the opposite propositions, to be called truths, with Arabic (19, etc.)

XIX. The Church is not a true and perfect society, altogether free, nor is she in possession of her own constant right conferred on her by the Divine Founder; but it belongs to the civil power to define what are the rights and what the limits of the Church, within which she may exercise the said rights.

19. The Church *of Rome is* a true and perfect society, altogether free. *She is in possession* of her own constant right, conferred on her by her Divine Founder, *and it does not* belong to the civil power to define what are the rights, *nor* what the limitations within which she may exercise the said rights.

XX. The ecclesiastical power ought not to exercise its authority without the permission and assent of the civil government.

20. The ecclesiastical power *ought* to exercise

its authority without the permission and *consent* of the civil government.

XXI. The Church has no power to define dogmatically that the religion of the Catholic Church is the only true religion.

21. The Church *of Rome has* power to define dogmatically that the religion of the *Roman* Church is the only true religion.

XXII. The obligation by which Catholic masters and writers are bound is confined to those things only which are set forth by the infallible judgment of the Church, as doctrines of faith to be believed by all men.

22. The obligation by which *Roman* Catholic masters and writers are bound is *not* confined to those things only which are set forth by the infallible judgment of *inspired writers*, as doctrines of faith to be believed by all men.

XXIII. Roman pontiffs and œcumenical councils have gone beyond the limits of their power, have usurped the rights of princes, and have also erred in defining matters of faith and manners.

23. Roman pontiffs and œcumenical councils have *never* gone beyond the limits of their power. They have *never* usurped the rights of princes, *neither have they* erred in defining matters of faith and manners.

XXIV. The Church has no right to employ force : she has not any temporal power, direct or indirect.

24. The Church has *the* right to employ force : she has *great* temporal power, *both* direct *and* indirect.

XXV. Besides the power inherent in the Episcopate, there is a temporal power which has been conceded to her, expressly or tacitly, by the civil authority, and consequently revocable at pleasure by this same civil authority.

25. Besides the *spiritual* power inherent in the *Roman* Episcopate, there is a temporal power which has been *acknowledged in* her, *both* expressly *and* tacitly, by the civil authority, and is *not revocable for any reason* by this same civil authority.

LXXVII. In our time it is no longer right that the Catholic religion should be regarded as the only religion of the State, to the exclusion of any other forms of worship.

77. At the present time *it continues to be* right that the *Romish* religion should be regarded as the only religion of the State, to the exclusion of *all other forms of worship*.

LXXVIII. Hence, to their praise be it spoken, in certain lands bearing the Catholic name, care is taken by the law that all men making their abode there be allowed the public exercise of their own worship.

78. Hence, to their praise be it spoken, in certain lands bearing the Catholic name, care is taken by the law that *no man whatever* making his abode there be allowed the public exercise of *his* own religion.

LXXIX. In fact, it is false that civil liberty for any form of worship, and also full power allowed to all for manifesting openly and publicly any opinions and any thoughts, conduces to the more easily corrupting people's manners and minds, and to propagating the pestilence of indifferentism.

79. In fact it is *true*, that civil liberty for any other form of worship, and *the least* power allowed *to any* person for manifesting, openly *or* publicly, any *other* opinions *or* any *other* thoughts conduces to the more easily corrupting people's manners and minds, and to propagating the pestilence of indifferentism.

LXXX. The Roman pontiff can and should reconcile himself with progress, and put himself in agreement with liberalism and recent civilization.

80. The Roman pontiff *neither can nor should* reconcile himself with progress, *nor* put himself in agreement with *liberty* and recent civilization.

Here, however, in this eightieth "truth," the Pope is quite right. Reconciliation is not possible, and ought not to be expected. Perhaps no Pope will have reigned longer than this vigorous father, Pius IX., and few have had a much more various and wide experience. He has made many trials of his own ability, and may be allowed to judge what a man in his position can be supposed able to do; and if he thinks that no Pope could reconcile himself with progress, nor keep up with the march of civilization, he must have credit for at least a grain of truth. Yet we have heard many eminent Romanists, when addressing strangers, boast the contrary. Be this as it may, the reader may now ponder the contradictions, determine for himself, and endeavour to estimate the consequences of such doctrine as this of the Pope, if it should find its way into our pulpits, our schools, and the press, and should even tinge, not to say *permeate*, the youthful mind of England.

INFALLIBILITY.

AT Pisa, or Constance, or Basil, no one would have ventured to propose that Papal infallibility should be counted a dogma of the faith. During

Infallibility. 67

the long schisms two pretended Popes, or three, or at one time five, by themselves or their proctors, would have had to cast lots for the prerogative, or Papal infallibility, like the Pagan goddess of Justia, must have taken flight, and found refuge in heaven, where only, after all, can there be exemption from error.

Whoever wishes to trace the figment of Papal infallibility to its source, must put himself under the guidance of industrious Ultramontanists, who can take him into the cells of mediæval obscurity, and find or invent some shreds of evidence that pontiffs have now and then been flattered by free councils with an ascription of infallibility. On the other hand, plain history tells another tale.

As the Council of the Vatican follows that of Trent as closely as possible, the Fathers of the Vatican may be expected to look to Trent for the latest and most available guidance. We therefore turn to Trent for authentic information of the doctrine of the Church of Rome, when last authentically expounded. Authority and wisdom are not inseparable companions, and no degree of authority can be taken to indicate a corresponding degree of wisdom. The decrees of Trent *de Reformatione* certainly invest the Pope with supreme administrative power; but even so, they all imply two pre-requisites; *one*, that the Pope should receive authentic information from the proper quarters, and *the other*, that the cardinals should be his constant counsellors in the administration of the laws of the Church, or assist his judgment in the reserved cases, which leave the Pope's will to be in the stead of law. Much of the wisdom which is wanted to assist his judgment, and much of the authority which is necessary to influence his will, is to be supplied by the cardinals. Nominally he is an absolute sovereign, but, in fact, his sovereignty is constitutionally moderated. The moderating power may be uncertain, but undoubtedly it exists. So much for his authority.

But wisdom is not to be meted by councillors to the *pontifex maximus* of Christian Rome. Hence the old question is to be settled, whether the Pope, speaking, as they say, *ex cathedrâ*, is infallible or not. Every one knows that outside Rome the majority are persuaded that he is not, but inside the Roman Court the majority would be glad if they might be persuaded that he is. A conciliar congregation *de fide* is now appointed, and it is expected that this great question—for *they* think it a very great question — will prove to have engaged their chief attention. " Henry Edward, Archbishop of Westminster," is on that congregation, and he has done all that he can do to prepare the mind of English Romanists for accepting the proposed new dogma, that whatever the Pope says *ex cathedrâ* will be as true as Gospel, and even more certain than that. On this point will the Council of Trent help the Council of the Vatican? Not in the least.

There is scarcely any allusion to the subject in the acts of Trent. Perhaps the nearest approach is in the chapter on the reservation of cases for absolution by the Pope alone (*Sessio* xiv., *De Pœnitentia*, cap. 7). It is to this effect:—
" It appeared to our most holy fathers most conducive to the discipline of Christian people that certain more atrocious and graver crimes should not be absolved by any but the chief priests. Wherefore the Popes, through the supreme power delivered to them in the universal Church, were able to reserve to their own judgment certain cases of graver crime. Nor is it to be doubted, since all things are ordained of God, that this is to all the bishops in their respective dioceses for edification, not for destruction, by the authority imparted to them over their subjects above other inferior priests, especially in respect to matters to which the censure of excommunication is attached. Now

it is consistent with Divine authority that this reservation of offences should be valid, not only in external polity, but also before God. But very piously, lest by this occasion any should perish in the Church of God, care was always taken that there should be no reservation in a man's dying moment, when all priests can absolve all penitents from all sins and censures whatsoever; but as, except at the last, the priests can do nothing in reserved cases, let them do their utmost to persuade penitents that they apply to the superior and legitimate judges for the benefit of absolution."

Now it is clear that, if the Council of Trent had believed the Pope to be infallible by virtue of his office, they would have thought him able to condemn a sinner even in the article of death; but lest, by occasion of the reservation of pardon to him alone, "any should perish," they would not allow him authority to withhold mercy from anyone in the article of death. They must have allowed it if they believe that the determination of giving or withholding absolution is to be left by Divine authority to the single judgment (*peculiari judicio*) of an infallible pontiff.

The theologians, bishops, and universities of France and Germany will have to consent or be coerced into obedience to the Ultramontane congregations and council if the proposed new dogma is proclaimed; but it is impossible to believe that they will consent, and it is certain that they cannot be compelled. This is all that we can say at present. History may not be anticipated, and it is not likely that any conjecture, hazarded as these pages pass through the press, would be in all respects justified by the event. At this moment the state of affairs is very critical.

In any event, we may be sure that no act of the Council can have any practical effect beyond what parties concerned may be willing to allow. No decision of the Council can anywhere have the force of law, nor can the members of the Council assume with success the language of authority. They of Trent presumed to say, even after half Europe had deserted them, "The holy synod exhorts all kings, princes, republics, and magistrates; and, in virtue of holy obedience, commands them that, as often as they are required, they be pleased to render their assistance and authority to the bishops, abbots, and generals aforesaid, and to other prefects, for the execution of the decree of reformation contained above; that, without any impediment, the decrees promised may be rightly executed to the praise of Almighty God "

(*Sessio* xxv., cap. 22). For the first time, then, in the whole course of Christian history, a Council has been held, having the name of "œcumenical," without the power of enacting a single law for the Church it undertakes to govern, or of calling in a single state in the world to support them, by enforcing the execution of their decrees.

So new a thing is this, that a Protestant would not make the statement without pausing for a moment to guard himself against exaggeration. Let us, therefore, borrow the language of an unquestionable authority, as Dr. Manning, in this case, must be considered. "What government," he asks, "at this day professes to be Catholic? . . . What country in Europe at this day recognises the unity and authority of the Catholic Church as a part of its public laws? What country has not, by royal edicts, or legislative enactments, or revolutionary changes, abolished the legal status of the Catholic Church within its territory? . . . As governments and nations, they have, by their own act, withdrawn themselves from the unity of the Church. As moral or legal persons, they are Catholic no longer" (*Pastoral Letter*, 1869, p. 127). The fact is simply this: that the separation of the states once called Catholic from the Church of

Rome has been gradual, and is not yet formally proclaimed. It is not a sudden schism, but a quiet desertion in consequence of indifference or disgust, and the meeting of a Council in self-declared separation from all states will not fail to be marked in history as the termination of a period—"the end of the things that have passed away," as Chrysostom says, when speaking of the destruction of Jerusalem, in the passage to which the Pope himself unwittingly directed our attention. We may now mark NICÆA as the first general council in which the civil power took a part, and TRENT as the last. Let the VATICAN stand at the opening of a new chapter, —not to say the last chapter, which would be unlikely,—in the history of the Papacy, which did not appear all at once, and is not likely to vanish at a stroke.

COUNCILS HELD IN ROME.

I CANNOT refrain from adding a brief note on the Councils hitherto holden in the city of Rome, and dignified with the title of Œcumenical. They have all been held in times of trouble or disgrace, were all entirely subject to the direct personal control of the Popes who convened them, and have been remarkably devoid of permanent influence, except for purposes of persecution. They stand thus:—

A.D. 1123.—Lateran I. called the Ninth Œcumenical. The Pope Calixtus II. published the decrees in his own name, as if the abbots and bishops present were of no account whatever. The object of the so-called Council was to inspirit the mass of the clergy everywhere against the secular authorities—to set the Pope above the king in every country. Not much came of it.

A.D. 1139.— Lateran II., Œcumenical X. Innocent II. convened and ruled as many bishops as he could get together, to denounce a rival with whom he had had a pitched battle. After this he had to flee from Rome, took refuge in France, was, like Pius IX., restored to Rome by a French army, and was kept in possession of the same, just as it happens at the present moment.

A.D. 1179.—Lateran III., Œcumenical XI. Alexander III. convened this assembly for the twofold purpose of guarding against the election of antipopes in future, but signally failed, and of putting down the Cathari, Patarenes, and other dissentients, but also with slight success, beyond the shedding of much blood. This third Lateran was called the Pope's Council, inasmuch as the whole business was transacted by him and for him.

A.D. 1215.—Lateran IV., Œcumenical XII. Innocent III. surrounded himself with 412 bishops, over whom he presided. Using this appearance of a Council, he engaged them to correct bad manners—a favourite occupation of pontiffs, who have always much unfinished work of the kind in hand—and to condemn heretics. In this Council he laid broad and sure foundations for the full establishment of the Inquisition, for which preparatory measures had been taken by Alexander in the preceding council of the Lateran. Here he bound princes and magistrates to kill those whom the Inquisitors should condemn.

A.D. 1512 to 1517.—Lateran V., Œcumenical XIX. Julius II. began this Council to strengthen himself against Louis XII. of France, who had invaded Italy. Leo X. continued it in order to follow up the same object, and, as he professed, maintain peace among the princes of Christendom, many of whom, however, were effectually alienated from the papacy by his own extravagances. He did his best to nullify those regulations of the Council of Pisa, which gave councils authority over Popes, made the Council declare absolutely the contrary, and denounced solemn excommunication upon all persons who should presume to comment upon, or interpret its transactions, without the special licence of the Holy See.

A.D. 1869. . . . This council has not yet received its name, nor done its work, but answers exactly to the character of all that have preceded it in the same city.

PROBABLE EFFECTS OF THIS LAST COUNCIL.

In England and throughout the British empire, as well as in the United States of America, some marked results of this Council may be reasonably expected. Already it presents Romanism to public view under an aspect which has not generally drawn sufficient attention. The reports daily received from Rome during the preparatory ceremonies, the books previously written in France and Germany, and the speculations excited on many interesting topics, have led to new trains of thought, and to fresh and unexpected anticipations. If all this leads to broad historic views of the whole subject, and raises writers and speakers above the low ground of controversy on small points and personalities, great good will follow.

Already earnest prayer—but, we must hope, not presumptuous nor imprecatory—has been offered, and cannot be offered in vain. Let the anathemas of Trent, the curses launched ages before and ages after, and the contemptuous bitterness of priestly writers of the straiter sect of Ultramontanists, where they have not provoked excessive indignation, now call forth blessing as the only fit answer to revilings; and if prayer and blessings abound on our side, both they and we shall have eventually great cause of satisfaction. The possibility that the Council may be prolonged for a few months at least gives hope that earnest Christian people, and especially such as lead public opinion in the pulpit and by the press, will learn and profit much, without suffering the injurious irritation of private controversy.

The worst effect on ourselves, not so much of the Council as of the general disfavour into which the Papacy has fallen on the continent of Europe, is felt already in the rapid influx of Romanism from other countries. Some of the most important Romish missionary and educational institutions are planting their establishments in England, and the religion which, fifty years ago, was alien, almost unknown, and regarded with a kind of traditional horror, now makes itself almost everywhere familiar. There is a false impression that this rapid increase of congregations, schools, brotherhoods, and sisterhoods, is all of English growth, or nearly all. The large outlay of cash in many directions, independently of local resources (which are comparatively small), occasions an impression of great wealth, and naturally provokes the suspicion that Protestant liberality has contributed largely to this new prosperity. The suspicion is not altogether groundless, but it is exaggerated. The assemblage of a Council in Rome, carried on from month to month, scowling with defiance on united Italy, and acting in concert with the ex-king of the two Sicilies and some lesser Italian princes, and other unseated potentates, looks so much like a political demonstration against the states that were under despotic government twenty years ago, that the priestly party are in a worse and worse position every day, and their immigrants necessarily multiply in our country. This is the very worst effect of the Council of the Vatican; or, if turned to good account, it may actually be the best. If these people flock hither for an asylum, and so become our neighbours, we must make them our friends too, and lead them, God helping us, to the Head of the Church, our Great High Priest, who sits enthroned among us, as we trust He does, and will show the tokens of His presence.

An effort to do this would bring us to the Bible, which our scholars and even our preachers have studied far too little. They will probably bring with them more unbelief than superstition, and compel us again to feel after the half-forgotten foundations of our faith. In exchange for the asylum we afford them in common with other fugitives, we shall, of course, assert our right to collect congregations and erect churches in all the cities in Europe, specially in the south, and prove to them, if they have not yet learned to confess it, that ours is no mere insular religion, but the catholic worship and confession of the triune God. They must know, that from the rising to the setting sun our brethren bow the knee, and confess that Christ is Lord, to the glory of the Father.

We cannot indulge them here with a very large enjoyment of their secret. We have no inquisitions, and we hate confessionals. They must not promise themselves the convenience of monastic prisons, nor expect their nunneries to be always barred against the light of day, nor hope to have cursing-places near their altars, nor to be allowed control over the press, nor wish us to leave them the shelter of latitudinarian silence; but they shall have honest English liberty, and we will retain and use the same.

On the Continent, and in more distant lands where the religion of Rome has hitherto been associated with the State, and until very lately dominant, the changes must be great.

The ostentatiously sacerdotal Council lately opened in Rome will necessarily be the pattern for diocesan synods, if they have them, and provincial or national councils, if they think it practicable and desirable to hold them, all independent of the State. But every such assemblage will be a practical proclamation of the separation of the Church of Rome from all states in the world. The chief men of the town will not carry a silken canopy over the head of the metropolitan, or other pontiff, as he rides along their street on a gentle mule, shod with golden shoes. The rule of the bishops' ceremonial will not be kept.

Better still, the national spirit will rise above the Roman. Rome may return to Italy, but Italy will no longer crouch to Rome. If the Council of the Vatican confirms the Syllabus, and declares the Pope infallible, Italy will consider how she may most gracefully demonstrate the mistake. Spain, in that case, may be provoked to take down the Papal arms from the palace of the Nuncio, and France, withdrawing her soldiers from what was once the Papal territory, may go on quietly by herself, and leave any successors that may come after Pius IX. to follow their own course, so long as they, too, will go on quietly.

The national spirit will now inevitably revive. Sovereigns and parliaments will so shape the laws as to lower the claims of the clergy in regard to immunities from civil charges, and the tenure of Church property. Society at large will encourage the priesthood to cast off the degrading yoke of celibacy. The episcopal oath will be everywhere abolished, because it is everywhere inconsistent with regal rights and national independence. Popes used to launch interdicts upon nations, shut up the churches, muffle the bells, leave the living unblest and the dead unburied, until princes wrapped themselves in sackcloth, did penance, and on bared knees implored mercy of the man who boasted himself God's vicegerent upon earth. Now, nations will put their interdict upon the Papacy, if the Papacy is not careful to refrain from provocation. They have already intimated, after careful deliberation in the Cabinets, that their dealing towards Rome, self-separated from their company, will, for the present at least, depend upon the doings of this Council.

In the line taken by the Pope who summoned the Council, and who rules it, there is nothing conciliatory to the governments; and unless he proves his fallibility and good sense at the same time by cancelling all his Allocutions and Letters Apostolic, and Encyclicals, recanting all his hard speeches and contemptuous threats, and bidding his Council help him to be gracious, the Government will indeed turn an interdict upon the Ultramontane priesthood, and leave him or his successors to shiver in the cold of a universal political desertion.

There was a certain charm during the first week or so, of conciliar spectacles and entertainments. St. Peter's Cathedral served well as a place of meeting for ecclesiastics and foreign notabilities of the lesser grades. A judicious mingling of titular bishops and patriarchs from the East, with Pope's guards and cardinals, impressed less-informed strangers with a notion of world-wide reverence for the aged priest-king whom they saw carried on his gestatory chair, or seated on his throne. But the processions are over. The music is silent. The bishops are broaching their opinions. Even cardinals give signs of discontent. The attendance is felt to be compulsory. The Court of Rome has lost its ancient splendour, and the visitors cannot help observing that the Pope is not supported by men of commanding talent and influence in the Courts of Europe. He is too much alone. The stars around him are of too little magnitude. The senator of Rome is nobody. The people of Rome are nothing. Italy is too far off. The brigands are too important. People are all strangers; even the Pope has lived too long. The Romans are counting his days, and, in spite of history, begin to fancy that in longevity he may even equal or exceed St. Peter, first Pope regnant in the Eternal City, whose length of reign no Pope has ever quite equalled. All this, indeed, about Peter, first of Popes, is grossly fabulous; but it is no illusion that Pius IX. must soon die, and unless sufficient grief can be simulated at his exequies, he will depart unwept.

The prospect is very gloomy. But when, nearly a quarter of a century ago, Pius was crowned, a tuft of tow was ceremonially consumed before him, and when it was reduced to ashes, a servant of the palace cried, as was the custom, *Sancte Pater. Sic transit gloria mundi.* ("Holy Father. Thus passes away the glory of the world.") Thus indeed it passes. Thus passed away the last of the Roman Emperors. Thus will, some day, the last of the Popes pass off the stage where this one has played a stubborn part. They may linger for a time, just like the Knights of Malta in San Giovanni, but, like the Caliphs of Bagdad and Cordova, those true successors of Mohammed, these counterfeit vicars of Christ will pass away into the limbus of oblivion.

Hodder & Stoughton's New Works in Theology.

Lectures on the First and Second Epistles of Peter. By the Rev. JOHN LILLIE, D.D., Author of "Lectures on the Epistle of Paul to the Thessalonians," &c. With a Preface by PHILIP SCHAFF, D.D. In 8vo, 12s. cloth.

Masterpieces of Pulpit Eloquence, Ancient and Modern. With Historical Sketches of Preaching in the different Countries represented, and Biographical and Critical Notices of the several Preachers and their Discourses. By HENRY C. FISH, D.D. In 2 vols, 8vo, 21s. cloth.

The History of the Church in the Eighteenth and Nineteenth Centuries. By K. R. HAGENBACH, D.D., Professor of Theology in the University of Basle. Translated by JOHN E. HURST, D.D. In 2 vols. 8vo, 24s. cloth.

The State of the Blessed Dead. Advent Sermons. By the Very Rev. HENRY ALFORD, D.D., Dean of Canterbury. Square 16mo, 1s. 6d. cloth.

St. Mark's Gospel. A New Translation, with Notes and Practical Lessons. By Professor J. H. GODWIN, New College. Cr. 8vo, 4s. 6d. cloth.

A Homiletic Analysis of the Gospel according to Matthew. By JOSEPH PARKER, D.D., Author of "Ecce Deus," &c. With an Introductory Essay on the Life of Jesus Christ, considered as an Appeal to the Imagination. Crown 8vo, 7s. 6d. cloth.

The Prophecies of our Lord and His Apostles. A Series of Discourses delivered in the Cathedral Church of Berlin. By W. HOFFMANN, D.D., Chaplain in Ordinary to the King of Prussia. In crown 8vo, 7s. 6d. cloth.

HODDER & STOUGHTON, 27, PATERNOSTER ROW.

THE ŒCUMENICAL COUNCIL.

Now Ready, price Fourpence.

The Call of the Hour. By the Rev. W. Guest, Author of "The Young Man Setting Out in Life."

NEW BOOK FOR THE TIMES.

Elegantly bound in cloth, with Nine full-page Illustrations, crown 8vo, price 7s. 6d.

Priest and Nun. A Story of Convent Life.

"'Priest and Nun' is a tale intended to bring out the secrets of convent life. It removes that veil which makes convent life so attractive to the ignorant and sentimental. The true history has been brought out lately in the notorious trial in this country and in the infamous Cracow case. This book is strictly based on facts, no statement being made that cannot be justified by actual history. The story is kept up with interest. It is just the kind of book to present to young people at a time when the Church of Rome, and her imitators in the Church of England, are doing all in their power to allure back the people to those heathenish superstitions which utterly pervert Christianity."—*Christian Work.*

"It is evidently, as it purports to be, a tale of real life, cleverly exposing the insidious principles of the Romish Church and giving a true picture of the inner life of the modern nunnery."—*Literary World.*

"Doubtless the accusation of exaggeration will be hurled against so fearful an exposure as this book unhesitatingly makes of the conduct adopted and carried out in convent life. But 'facts are stubborn things,' and we have no more doubt that we here meet with the revelation of positive facts than we have of our own existence."—*Bell's Weekly Messenger.*

HODDER & STOUGHTON, 27, PATERNOSTER ROW.

New Work by Dr. Pressensé.

The Early Years of Christianity. By E.
DE PRESSENSÉ, D.D. A Sequel to "Jesus Christ: His Times, Life, and Work." Just published, in 8vo, price 12s. cloth.

"The lofty and animated eloquence which he has always at command, and a certain happy faculty of finding, even in doctrinal discussions, some picturesque trait, some feature with life and colour, have enabled him to overcome the difficulties which stand in the way of a popular history of the Christian life and literature of the first century." — *Contemporary Review.*"

"The volume forms one of the best helps to the study of the Acts of the Apostles, and indeed of all the succeeding portions of the New Testament. The translation is admirably executed."—*Pulpit Analyst.*

WORKS BY THE SAME AUTHOR.

Jesus Christ: His Times, Life, and Work.
Third and Cheaper Edition. Crown 8vo, price 9s. cloth.

"M. de Pressensé is not only brilliant and epigrammatic, but his sentences flow on from page to page with a sustained eloquence which never wearies the reader. The Life of Christ is more dramatically unfolded in this volume than in any other work with which we are acquainted."—*Spectator.*

The Mystery of Suffering, and other Discourses.
New Edition. In crown 8vo, price 3s. 6d. cloth.

The Land of the Gospel: Notes of a
Journey in the East. In crown 8vo, 5s. cloth.

The Church and the French Revolution.
A History of the Relations of Church and State from 1789 to 1802. In crown 8vo, 9s. cloth.

HODDER & STOUGHTON, 27, PATERNOSTER ROW.

Mr. Paxton Hood's New Work.

Now Ready, in One handsome Volume, 700 pp. crown 8vo, cloth, red edges, price 10s. 6d.

The World of Anecdote: an Accumulation
of Facts, Incidents, and Illustrations—Historical and Biographical—from Books and Times, Recent and Remote. By EDWIN PAXTON HOOD.

BY THE SAME AUTHOR.

Second Thousand, price 10s. 6d., handsomely bound, uniform with the above.

Lamps, Pitchers, and Trumpets: Lectures
on the Vocation of the Preacher. Illustrated by Anecdotes—Biographical, Historical, and Elucidatory—of every Order of Pulpit Eloquence, from the great Preachers of all ages.

"A book which we cordially recommend to all who take any interest in preaching. The book is a most valuable one, interesting as a romance, and quite unique in its kind." *Dublin University Magazine.*

"Fresh, clever, sensible, and full of stimulus and thought for men aspiring to preach. The genius and power of the pulpit are vindicated, its character is pointed out, and the faults and merits of sermons are touched with a keen and racy criticism, and in the generous spirit of a man of large sympathies and culture. An excellent feature of these lectures is their copiousness of illustration; and the carefully-studied and picturesque monographs, ranging from Chrysostom and St. Bernard down to Lacordaire and Robertson, are full of interest." —*Christian Work.*

HODDER & STOUGHTON, 27, PATERNOSTER ROW.

John, Charles, Samuel, and Susannah Wesley.

Now Ready, crown 8vo, 3s. 6d. cloth.

Anecdotes of the Wesleys. By the Rev J. B. WAKELEY.

"There is not one page of the book without interest. Samuel Wesley, sen., Susannah Wesley, Charles Wesley, and Samuel Wesley, jun., are all brought before us in sprightly form; but John Wesley fittingly receives the largest attention."—*Watchman.*

"Is a book likely to be a great favourite, for Mr. Wakeley has given us a very happy assortment of anecdotes illustrating the character of the famous brothers."—*John Bull.*

"To all Wesleyans and to many not of that persuasion this book will be very acceptable. There are nearly 400 anecdotes relating to different members of the Wesley family—29 to Samuel Wesley, 20 to his wife Susannah, no less than 282 to John Wesley, 67 to Charles Wesley, and 5 to Charles Wesley, jun. The book gives us many pleasant sketches of the lives of that remarkable family, one member of which caused such a memorable movement in the English Church." *Daily Review.*

"These anecdotes are well selected. We see pictured forth in them the extraordinary divinely-directed career of these remarkable men. There are many of the most striking indications of the presence and care of God, even in the smallest concerns of life. This book is one which no earnest Christian can peruse without encouragement and benefit. It is sure to be universally popular."—*Christian Work.*

The Mother's Annual: Being the First
Volume of a New Illustrated Series of "The Mother's Friend." Beautifully illustrated, small 4to, neat boards, 1s. 6d. (Also, in cloth elegant, price 2s. 6d. gilt edges.)

HODDER & STOUGHTON, 27, PATERNOSTER ROW.

Small Books for Presentation.

Price 2s. each.

The Melody of the Twenty-third Psalm. By ANNA WARNER, one of the Authors of "The Wide, Wide World." Square 16mo.

The Heritage of Peace; or, Christ our Life. By T. S. CHILDS, D.D. Square 16mo.

Ancient Hymns and Poems; chiefly from St. Ephraem of Syria, Prudentius, Pope Gregory the First, and St. Bernard. Translated and imitated by the Rev. T. G. Crippen. Fcap. 8vo.

Price 1s. 6d. each.

The State of the Blessed Dead. Advent Sermons. By the Very Rev. HENRY ALFORD, D.D., Dean of Canterbury. Square 16mo.

Wholesome Words; or, Choice Passages from Old Authors. Selected and arranged by J. E. RYLAND, M.A. Fcap. 8vo.

The Young Man Setting out in Life. By Rev. W. GUEST, F.G.S. Third edition. Fcap. 8vo.

Price 1s. each.

Around the Cross. By N. ADAMS, D.D.

Meditations on the Lord's Supper. By the same.

Affliction; or, the Refiner Watching the Crucible. By Rev. CHARLES STANFORD, Author of "Central Truths."

The Dying Saviour and the Gipsy Girl. By MARIE SIBREE.

The Secret Disciple encouraged to avow his Master. By the late Rev. J. WATSON, of Hackney.

HODDER & STOUGHTON, 27, PATERNOSTER ROW.

www.ingramcontent.com/pod-product-compliance
Lightning Source LLC
Chambersburg PA
CBHW020257090426
42735CB00009B/1124